Saliha Sneezes

Mini Mu'min Du'a Series #13

www.Mini-Mumin.com

Copyright © 2012 Mini Mu'min Publications

All rights reserved. This publication may not be reproduced in whole or in part by any means whatsoever without written permission from the copyright owner.

Introduction

All praise is due to Allah the Most High, may Allah send His blessings on the Prophet Muhammad (saw), his family, his companions, and those who follow him in righteousness until the Day of Judgment.

"And remember your Lord by your tongue and within yourself, humbly and in awe, without loudness, by words in the morning and the afternoon, and be not among those who are neglectful." (Holy Qur'an 7:205)

The **Mini Mu'min Du'a Series** is designed to help you teach your child essential Islamic supplications and the situations in which they would be used. Each book focuses on a single topic, with key vocabulary **highlighted**. These key words can then serve as a tool to remind your child of important points. All supplications are shown in Arabic text, translation, and transliteration. For any assertions regarding fiqh we have provided textual proofs, from the Qur'an and authentic Sunnah of the Prophet (saw), at the bottom of the relevant page. Each story is accompanied by original artwork, but in accordance with Islamic beliefs we do not use human or animal images.

Transliteration has been provided here as a means to help those who do not know Arabic to teach supplications to their children. But it must be noted that all transliteration is imperfect and cannot accurately represent Arabic sounds in their entirety. We therefore encourage anyone who uses our books to use the transliteration as a tool, but not an end in itself, and to eventually learn the supplications in the original Arabic.

In some cases, sounds will be represented in the transliteration (because they are present in the Arabic text) that will not actually be pronounced. These generally occur at the end of a supplication and are related to the Arabic rules for pausing and stopping. To clarify this for non-Arabic speakers, we have placed brackets [ ] around those sounds in the transliteration that would not be pronounced when reciting the supplication.

Thank you for purchasing this book, may Allah benefit both you and your child through it, forgive us for any errors we have made, and benefit us in this life and the Hereafter if there is any good in it.

Saliha was busy building
The best sandcastle around,

In the big sandbox
At the school playground.

It had plenty of tall towers
And windows galore!

She was just getting ready
To add on some more…

When all of a sudden,
She felt a small itch-

Her nose felt funny,
It was starting to twitch…

She sniffed for a second,
Then she snuffed for two,

Then finally, she said…

"Achoo!"

She thought she was finished,
Her sneeze was all done-

Now she could get back
To her sandcastle fun.

But then she remembered,
There was something amiss,

A Muslim could never
Forget about this…

The Muslim says something-
Parts **one**, **two**, and **three**,

She couldn't remember…
What could they be?!

The **sneezer** says **two** parts
(The beginning and end)

But the middle part
Has to be said by a **friend**.

Saliha looked around-
What to do, where to go?

Then she saw Fatimah and thought,
Maybe she would know…

Fatimah was drawing flowers,
Using pretty colored sticks of chalk-

Saliha asked politely, as she sat down
Next to her on the sidewalk…

"Do you happen to know,
Could you tell me please…

What do we say
When we sneeze?"

Fatimah looked puzzled
And said, "I don't understand…

Don't you just cover
Your nose with your hand?"

"No," said Saliha with a sigh,
"That's not it at all…

There is something we **say**,
Something very **small**."

Then, Saliha saw Maryam
Swinging up to the sky-

Perhaps she would know,
It was certainly worth a try.

Saliha ran over to the swing set,
Maryam was going really fast,

So she called out her question
As Maryam *swooshed* past…

"Do you happen to know,
Could you tell me please…

What do we say
When we sneeze?"

Maryam swung past again-
Not one time but two,

Then she called back her answer,
"Can I have a tissue?"

"No," said Saliha sadly,
"That's not quite it you see,

It's not just **one** thing-
It's supposed to be **three**…"

Saliha walked off slowly
Wondering why no one knew?

If she didn't get an answer
Oh, what would she do!

Then Saliha looked up and saw
Hameed hanging on the high bar-

She shouted up her question,
Because he was so far…

Hameed scratched his head
And considered a bit…

"Subhaan-Allah," he suggested,
"Do you think that would fit?"

"Thank you for trying," said Saliha,
"But that's not what we do-

That's not what we say
When we go…"

Achoo!

Saliha was getting worried,
Time was running out!

Looking for someone to help her,
She wandered all about…

Suddenly, she spotted Khadijah
On the slide- slipping past.

Saliha met her at the bottom,
Then hopefully she asked…

"Do you happen to know,
Could you tell me please…

What do we say
When we sneeze?"

"Sure," answered Khadijah,
"I know exactly what to do…"

"If you like," she added cheerfully,
"I can teach it all to you!"

"Let's go and play on the seesaw,
You can ride along with me,

While I teach you all the parts[1]-
One, **two**, and of course **three**!"

---

[1] When one of you sneezes he should say, "*All praise is for Allah*" and his brother or companion should say to him, "*May Allah have mercy on you*" and he (i.e. the one who sneezed) replies back to him, "*May Allah guide you and set your affairs in order*." (Al-Bukhaari 7/125)

So they got on the seesaw together,
Happily riding up and down.

Khadijah started to explain,
As she lifted up off the ground-

"Since you are the **sneezer**,
You have to **start**…"

> اَلْحَمْدُ لِلَّهِ
>
> *"Alhamdu lillaah"*
>
> (All praise is for Allah.)

She said, "Is **your** part."

Saliha pushed off with her feet
And rose up on her ride,

As Khadijah came slowly
Back down on her side-

> يَرْحَمُكَ اللَّهُ
>
> "Yarhamukallaah"
>
> (May Allah have mercy on you.)

"Is the part **I must do**,"

"Because," she explained,
"This is part number **two**."

Up and down they went,
Each one taking their turn-

Saliha was surprised by how
These adi'yaa were so easy to learn!

"This last one," said Khadijah
"Is part number **three**,

Since I made **du'a** for **you**,
Now you make **du'a** for **me**!"

يَهْدِيكُمُ اللَّهُ وَ يُصْلِحُ بَالَكُمْ

*"Yahdeekumul-laahu
wa yuslihu baalakum"*

(May Allah guide you and
set your affairs in order.)

Khadijah said with a smile,
"That's it- that's the end!

When you **sneeze**, all you need,
Is your **adi'yaa** and a good **friend**!

Just like you can't ride a seesaw,
When you are the only one-

Sneezers need a little help,
To get their du'a done!"

So, Saliha taught Fatimah,
Maryam, and Hameed…

Because spreading knowledge
Is a very good deed!

Now they <u>all</u> know
What to say and what to do-

They know the adi'yaa[2] for sneezing,
And now you know them too!

---

[2] "Adi'yaa"- Arabic word meaning "supplications", plural form of the Arabic word "du'a".

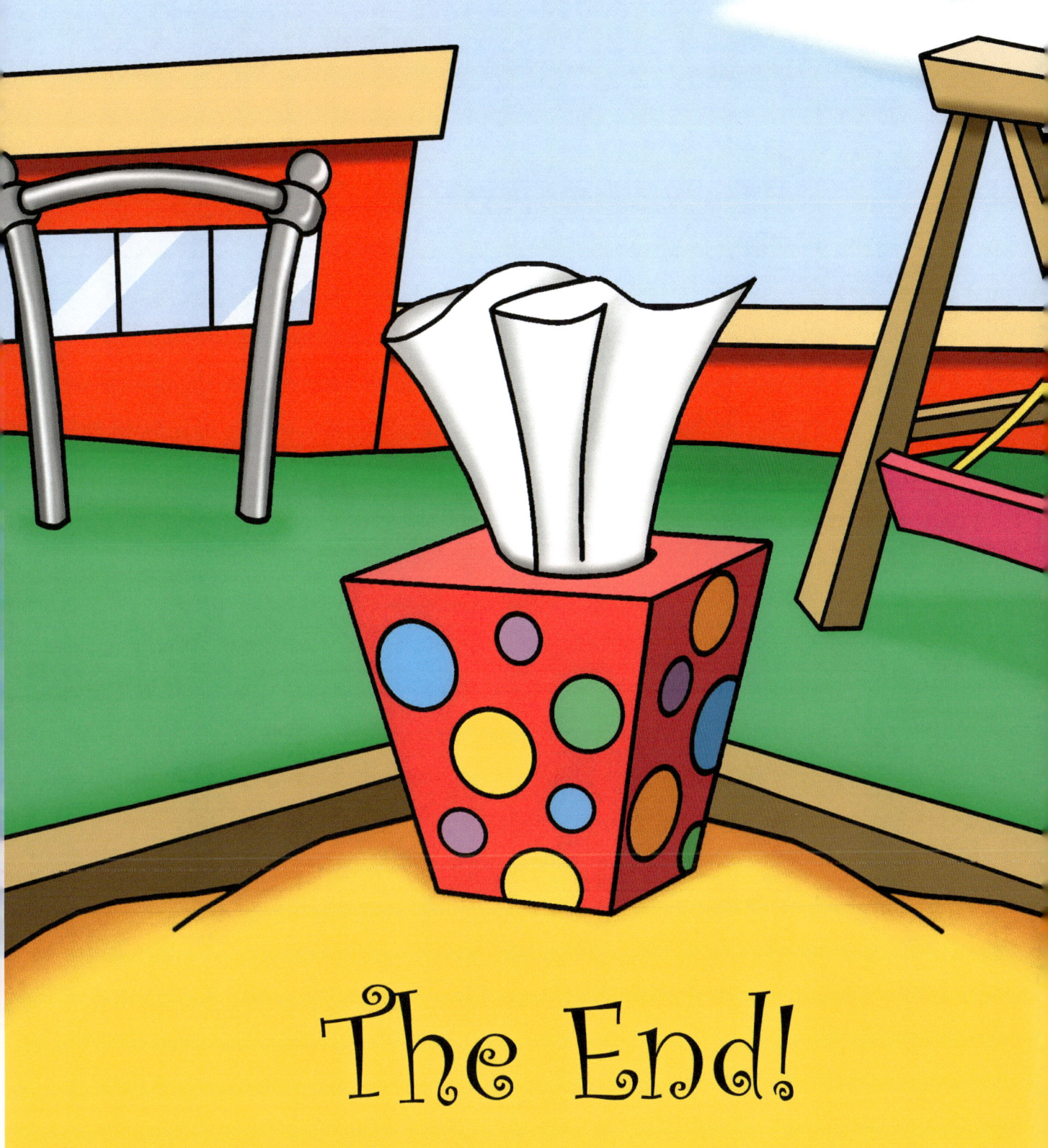

Other available titles in the Mini Mu'min Du'a Series:

Batool's Bedtime Story
Bilal's Bakery
Fatimah's First Fasting Day
Jameelah Gets Dressed
Muhammed Goes to the Masjid
Sajaad is Sick
Waheeda the Wudoo' Wonder
Waleed Wakes Up

and many more!...

Visit our online bookstore at:

www.Mini-Mumin.com

Made in the USA
Charleston, SC
13 January 2014